MEAN MACHINES
A SPOT-IT CHALLENGE

by Jennifer L. Marks

Capstone press
Mankato, Minnesota

A+ Books are published by Capstone Press,
151 Good Counsel Drive, P.O. Box 669, Mankato, Minnesota 56002.
www.capstonepress.com

1 2 3 4 5 6 14 13 12 11 10 09

Library of Congress Cataloging-in-Publication Data
Marks, Jennifer L., 1979–
 Mean machines : a spot-it challenge / by Jennifer L. Marks.
 p. cm. — (A+ books. Spot it)
 Includes bibliographical references and index.
 Summary: "Simple text invites the reader to find items hidden in vehicle-themed
photographs" — Provided by publisher.
 ISBN-13: 978-1-4296-2221-9 (hardcover)
 ISBN-10: 1-4296-2221-0 (hardcover)
 1. Picture puzzles — Juvenile literature. I. Title. II. Series.
GV1507.P47M272 2009
 793.73 — dc22   2008047476

Credits

Juliette Peters, set designer
Len Epstein, illustrator
All photos by Capstone Press Photo Studio.

Note to Parents, Teachers, and Librarians

Spot It is an interactive series that supports literacy development and reading enjoyment. Readers utilize visual discrimination skills to find objects among fun-to-peruse photographs with busy backgrounds. Readers also build vocabulary through thematic groupings, develop visual memory ability through repeated readings, and improve strategic and associative thinking skills by experimenting with different visual search methods.

The author dedicates this book to Aaron Wittrock of Savage, Minnesota. She was incredibly lucky
to find him.

Table of Contents

Burning Rubber

Can you spot. . .

- a letter J?
- a pliers?
- a red ribbon?
- a piano?
- a slice of pizza?
- a wire whisk?

5

Emergency, Emergency!

Can you spot. . .

- a chocolate sundae?
- a nurse's hat?
- a pink skirt?
- three dogs?
- a cup of tea?
- four bandage strips?

Kickin' Up Dust

Can you spot. . .
- a grasshopper?
- an orange?
- a paw print?
- a frog?
- a dollar sign?
- a red bead?

Let's Jet

Can you spot. . .
- a mustache?
- a Lego?
- a tugboat?
- a ghost?
- a sign for women?
- two bats?

School Bus Rush

Can you spot. . .

- a teddy bear?
- a golden crown?
- a pumpkin?
- a fork?
- four striped bees?
- a spare tire?

13

G.I. Spy

Can you spot. . .
- a clock?
- a nest of eggs?
- a camel?
- a wrench?
- a tarantula?
- a toy train?

Construction Junction

Can you spot. . .

- a penguin?
- a snowflake?
- a butterfly?
- a cat?
- two thermoses?
- the Statue of Liberty?

17

Out of This World!

Can you spot. . .

- an igloo?
- a bathtub?
- a milk jug?
- a jingle bell?
- three raccoons?
- a thimble?

KEYSTONE FARM

Edamame
SOYBEAN
delectable oriental favorite

The Tractor Factor

Can you spot. . .

- a red caboose?
- a tourist?
- two watering cans?
- a plate of cookies?
- a Thanksgiving turkey?
- a gray porcupine?

21

In Ship Shape

Can you spot. . .

- a mermaid?
- two skulls?
- a treasure chest?
- two scuba divers?
- a lighthouse?
- a blue life jacket?

23

Can I Get a Choo-Choo?

Can you spot. . .

- a take-out box?
- a picket fence?
- a high-fiving hand?
- five astronauts?
- a five-gallon pail?
- a pair of red shoes?

wesson.

UNION PACIFIC RAILROAD

UP 17042

STOP

Chases Dirt

Old Dutch Cleanser

BURLINGTON NORTHERN

From the Block

Can you spot. . .

- a camera?
- a battery?
- a trash can?
- an old TV?
- a clock?
- toaster?

Spot Even More!

Burning Rubber
4

Try to find a clover, a safety pin, a flower, a hatchet, a hammer, a saxophone, a hot dog, and a sea star.

Emergency, Emergency!
6

See if you can spot a pair of rubber boots, a red button, two fire extinguishers, and a thermometer.

Kickin' Up Dust
8

Take another look and find a green spider, a palm tree, a red car, a saddle, a football helmet, and a heart.

Let's Jet
10

Now find a pirate ship, an eraser, a hot air balloon, a spell book, a toucan, a letter L, and an oar.

School Bus Rush
12

Now spot a dump truck, a bottle of tanning oil, a yellow crayon, a shining sun, and a fish.

G.I. Spy
14

Try to spy a crocodile, a football, a gingerbread man, a cowboy hat, army dog tags, and a teddy bear.

Construction Junction

See if you can spy a spider web, a gray horn, a carrot, a horseshoe, two shovels, and an orange car.

Out of This World!

Try to find an elephant, a white shoe, a black shoe, a glittery moon, and eleven American flags.

The Tractor Factor

Now spot a bone, a sea star, some cow tracks, an orange button, a life jacket, a coffee pot, and three airplanes.

In Ship Shape

Try to find two blue eyes, two toothy mouths, a pair of sandals, a red flag, and three pincers.

Can I Get a Choo-Choo?

Now look for a rooster, a top hat, an arctic fox, a monster truck, green sunglasses, and two soldiers.

From the Block

Take one last look to find a white thumbtack, a gold jack, two cookie cutters, a motorcycle, and a silver car.

Extreme Spot-It Challenge

Just can't get enough Spot-It action? Try this extra challenge. See if you can spot:

- a blue convertible
- two stop signs
- a tree
- a key
- a safari jeep
- a bumble bee
- a blimp
- a jet ski
- a white convertible
- a blue van
- a saw
- a spare tire
- a bowling pin
- a red barn
- an anchor
- a covered wagon
- a moon rover

Read More

Kidslabel. *Spooky. Spot 7. Seek & Find.* San Francisco: Chronicle, 2007.

Marks, Jennifer L. *School Times: A Spot-It Challenge.* Spot It. Mankato, Minn.: Capstone Press, 2009.

Marzollo, Jean. *I Spy Little Wheels.* New York: Scholastic, 1998.

Internet Sites

FactHound offers a safe, fun way to find educator-approved Internet sites related to this book.

Here's what you do:
1. Visit *www.facthound.com*
2. Choose your grade level.
3. Begin your search.

This book's ID number is 9781429622219.

FactHound will fetch the best sites for you!